I AIN'T GONNA STUDY WAR NO MORE

Traditional

* The original melody, shown in small notes, requires a difficult jump from the 6th to the 1st position.

THE SIDEWALKS OF NEW YORK

CRADLE SONG

ON TOP OF OLD SMOKY

MR. FROG WENT A-COURTING

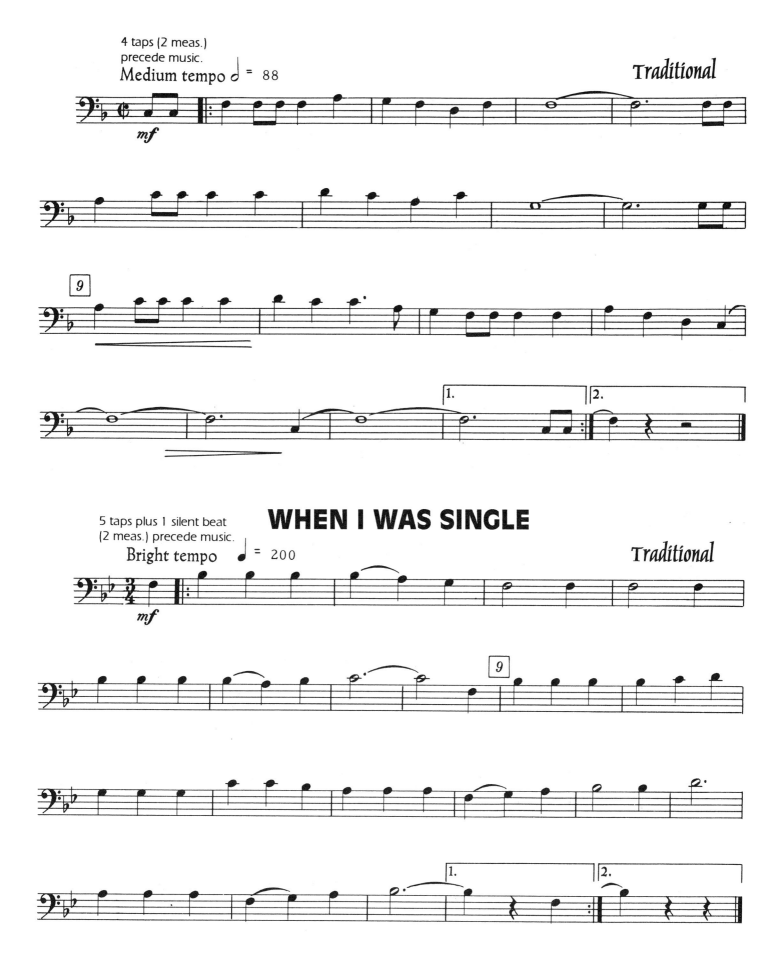

WHEN I WAS SINGLE

FIREPROOF POLKA

Joseph Strauss

OLD PAINT

GREENSLEEVES

YOU TELL ME YOUR DREAM

Charles N. Daniels

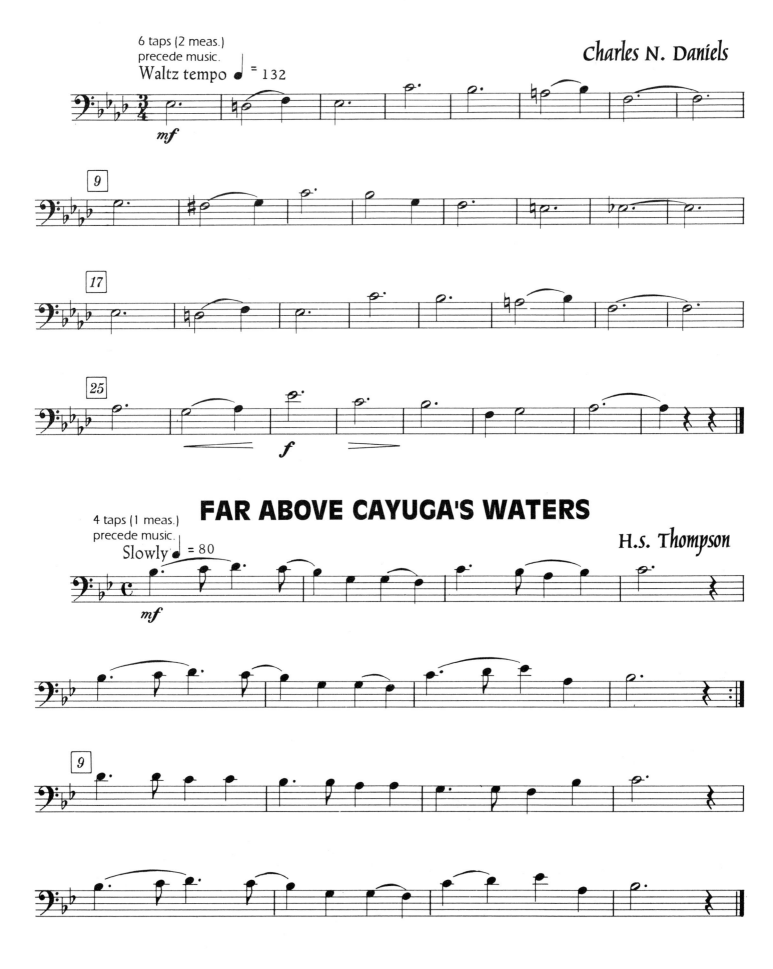

FAR ABOVE CAYUGA'S WATERS

H.S. Thompson

SPANISH GUITAR

College Song

Lively waltz ♩ = 192

CARELESS LOVE

WHEN THE SAINTS GO MARCHING IN

LITTLE BROWN JUG

4 taps (2 meas.)
precede music.

Eastburn

12

BLUES IN E-FLAT

Jay Arnold

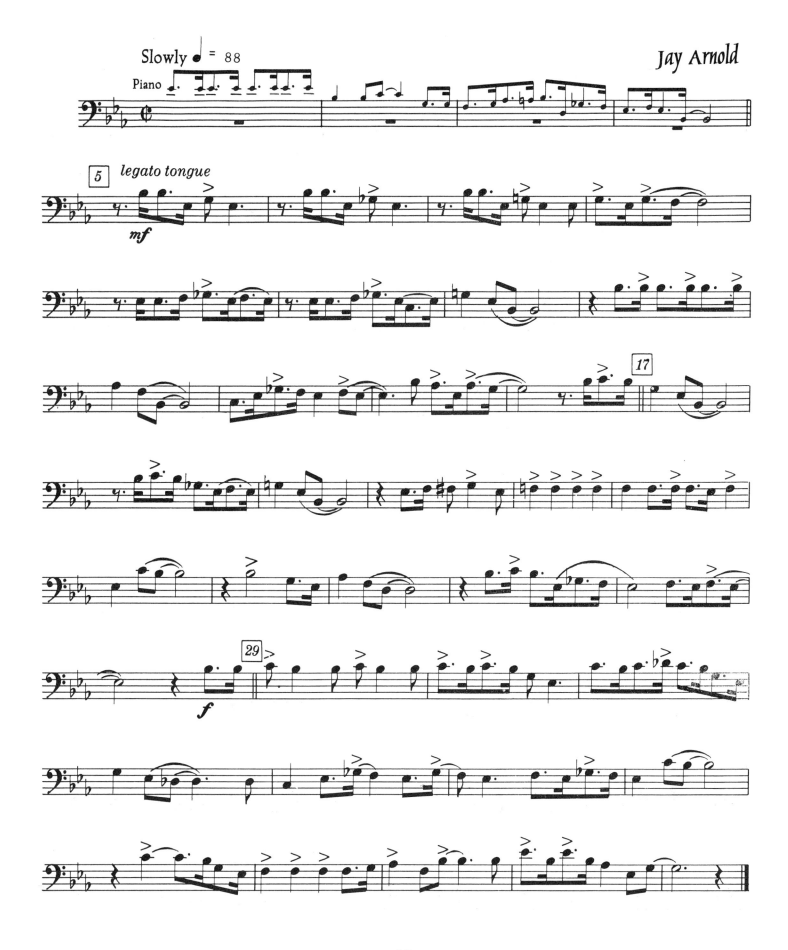

HELLO! MA BABY

BLACK IS THE COLOR OF MY TRUE LOVE'S HAIR

JESU, JOY OF MAN'S DESIRING

H. M. S. PINAFORE

Sir Arthur Sullivan

17

PETER AND THE WOLF

4 taps (1 meas.)
precede music.

PETER'S THEME
Moderato ♩ = 100

Serge Prokofieff

THE CAT'S THEME

THE WOLF'S THEME

THE HIGH SCHOOL CADETS

4 taps (2 meas.)
precede music.

𝅝 = 120

John Philip Sousa

Trio

MANHATTAN BEACH

THE RIFLE REGIMENT

THE COSSACK

Traditional Russian Melody

RECRUITING SONG
from "GYPSY BARON"

Johann Strauss

THEME FROM "MOLDAU"

Bedrich Smetana

MELODY FROM "PRINCE IGOR"

Moderato ♩ = 58

Alexander Borodin

THE YOUNG PRINCE AND THE YOUNG PRINCESS

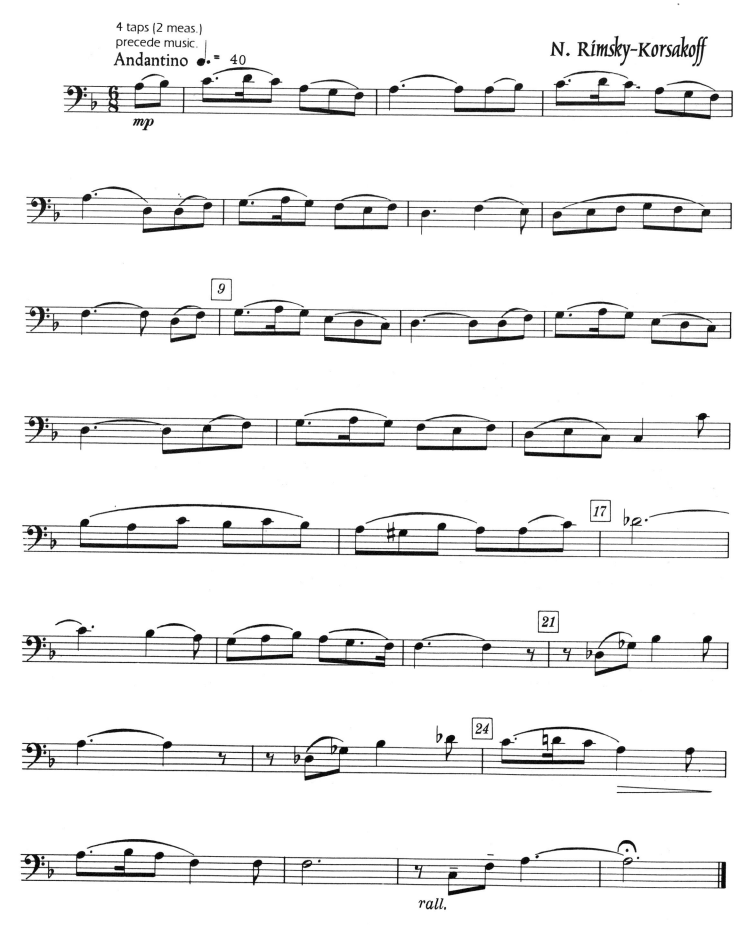

SCENE FROM "BLUEBEARD"

SCHEHERAZADE

from "ALBUM FOR THE YOUNG"

THE STARS AND STRIPES FOREVER

John Philip Sousa

TOREADOR SONG
from "CARMEN"

G. Bizet

28

BERCEUSE

from "L'OISEAU DE FEU"

Igor Stravinsky

NOCTURNE

MODERATO CON MOTO

from 'CLARINET SONATA, Op. 120"

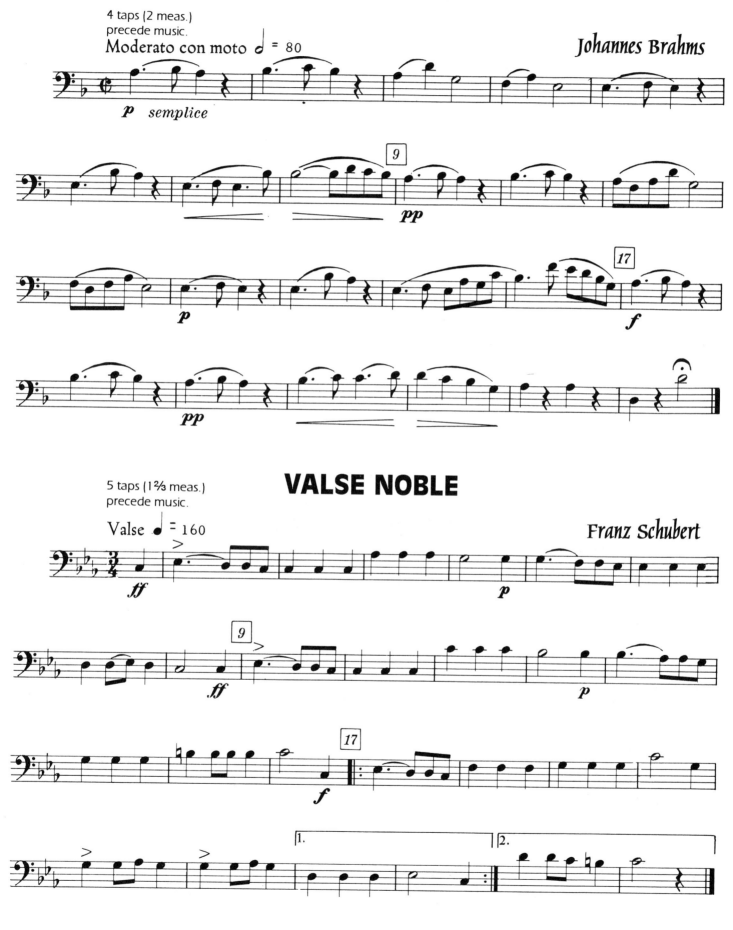

Johannes Brahms

VALSE NOBLE

Franz Schubert

IN DULCI JUBILO

CHORALE No.83